WOMEN
IN HISTORY

WOMEN AND SCIENCE

Brenda Clarke

Wayland

WOMEN
IN HISTORY

Women and Business
Women and Education
Women and Literature
Women and Politics
Women and Science
Women and Sport
Women and the Arts
Women and the Family
Women and War
Women and Work

Series Editor: Amanda Earl
Editor: Jannet King
Designer: Joyce Chester
Picture Editor: Shelley Noronha

Front cover: Laboratory of Natural Sciences, Girton College, Cambridge, 1921.
Back cover: Top left – Mary Somerville, mathematician (1780–1872). Top right – Elizabeth Garrett Anderson, doctor (1836–1917). Bottom left – Caroline Herschel, astronomer (1750–1848) (from a portrait painted in 1829 by Martin François Tielmans). Bottom right – Mary Leakey, archaeologist and anthropologist (b.1913).

British Library Cataloguing in Publication Data
Clarke, Brenda, *1946–*
    Women and science
    1. Science. Role of women 2. Medicine. Role of women
    I. Title II. Series
    509

    ISBN 1–85210–390–6

First published in 1989
by Wayland (Publishers) Ltd
61 Western Road, Hove,
East Sussex BN3 1JD, England

Typeset by Kalligraphics Limited, Horley, Surrey
Printed in Italy by G. Canale & C.S.p.A., Turin
Bound in the UK by Mac Lehose & Partners, Portsmouth

Picture acknowledgements
The pictures in this book were supplied by the following: Aldus Archive 9, 14; Ann Ronan: back cover (bottom left), 4, 5, 7 (top and bottom), 24 (top); Bruce Coleman 37 (bottom); Camera Press 29 (top), 41; ET Archive 29 (bottom); Format 37 (top), 40, 43, 45; Girton College Archive: front cover, 18, 35; Hulton Picture Library: back cover (top left and top right), 6, 13, 15 (bottom left), 23, 25 (top and bottom), 27, 28, 30, 31, 36; Mansell Collection 32; Mary Evans Picture Library 8, 10, 11, 12, 15 (bottom right and top), 16, 17, 19, 20, 22, 24, 26, 33, 34 (top and bottom); Philip Ollerenshaw 44; Popperfoto: back cover (bottom right), 38; Royal Botanical Gardens, Kew 20, 21. The artwork on page 42 was supplied by Thames Cartographic Services.

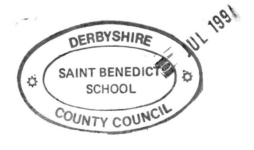

Contents

Introduction

Goddesses of healing and health were common in ancient societies, as it was women who cared for the sick. Hygeia, Greek goddess of health, was often pictured with a serpent, sometimes shown drinking from her hand. From Hygeia's name comes our word 'hygiene'.

'

I was out driving once with an old farmer in Vermont . . .'You women may talk about your rights, but why don't you invent something?' I answered, 'Your horse's feed bag and the shade over his head were both of them invented by women.' Ada C. Bowles, quoted by H.J. Mozans in *Women in Science*, 1913

'

When did the link between women and science begin? Who were the first women scientists? Few people could answer either question with certainty, and if they looked at a general history of science, they would probably be none the wiser.

Most authorities agree that the science of the Western world began with the philosophers of Ancient Greece. They tried to explain the natural wonders of the world by observing and recording what was happening around them, and then organizing their new knowledge into scientific theories. They were the first 'research' scientists.

Yet science and technology (the way science is put into practice) existed long before the Greeks, with tool-making, hunting, cooking, weaving, pottery, building and farming. The history of science charts human progress.

People have therefore been scientists from the earliest times – and many vital scientific tasks have been carried out by women. It was they who took care of the sick, and of women in childbirth. They gathered herbs, mixed medicines and handed on their knowledge to the next generation. In fact, people in many early civilizations prayed to goddesses in times of sickness – which shows how healing was associated with female skill.

Civilization could not have developed without agriculture, and farming was almost certainly first carried out by women. Stories, traditions and legends have linked goddesses with the invention of agricultural tools, processes such as pressing olives for oil, and with crafts of various kinds. It is easy to imagine how advances in technology (needles, the pestle and mortar, the loom, the potter's wheel) came about as women sewed skins, grew and harvested plants, ground grain and made cloth and cooking pots.

As farming and towns developed, societies became more complex and organized. Other sciences were needed: mathematics for accurate measurement and astronomy to prepare calendars. But as society changed, women lost many of their opportunities for technological invention. Now professional potters, weavers and builders took charge of industrial production, and they were

mostly men. Of the special skills associated with women, that of healing remained longest in their hands.

This cycle seems to have been repeated many times, wherever civilizations grew, flourished and declined. We know that in ancient Mesopotamia and Egypt, women were active in astronomy, in medicine (before 3000 BC) as physicians and surgeons, and as chemists. There were women scientists, too, in Ancient Greece. But we know little of them now.

So, apart from Marie Curie, the one female scientist everyone can name, has any woman of modern times achieved anything significant in science? It is hard to think of any women inventors, for example. But there have been some. They may have lacked the money to see their inventions become reality; they may have been forced to hand them over to others, or (denied education at university and the practical experience of the workshop) they may have asked men to convert their ideas into actual constructions.

A famous example is that of the mechanical cotton gin, invented (so reference books tell us) by Eli Whitney in 1793. But the idea was that of fellow American Mrs Catherine Greene (1755–1814),

An Egyptian painting of c.970 BC shows women ploughing and reaping. Even before this time, women had gathered wild cereals, using their knowledge of these crops in the development of farming.

❛ *She sold the invention to an agent . . . in 1888. The wringer is a great financial success . . . When asked . . . why she sold the invention so cheap after giving months of study to it, she replied, 'You know I am black and if it was known that a Negro woman patented the invention, white ladies would not buy the wringer.'* Ellen Eglin, a black charwoman described in *The Woman Inventor*, 1890 ❜

Right *Marie Curie, discoverer of radium, was the first scientist to be awarded two Nobel Prizes.*

who encouraged Whitney to build the machine, and helped him to improve its design. Most inventions by women are practical like this, designed to make everyday life and work easier.

We know of few female scientists today because only recently did anyone think of looking for them. And it is difficult to trace their work: so often it was absorbed into that of the men with whom they worked, who published it as theirs. The conventional picture of women in science is therefore that of white-coated laboratory assistants, even though we know that women are doctors, engineers, physicists and research chemists, and that they win Nobel Prizes.

1

From Alchemy to Enlightenment

350 BC–1800

A woman working the bellows to heat the furnace of a still, from a book printed in 1514.

Modern science is usually considered to have started in 1543, when Copernicus published his revolutionary idea that the universe centred on the Sun, not the Earth. So ended the long-standing view of the world as described by Ptolemy of Alexandria in the second century AD.

The city of Alexandria (North Africa) had been founded by Alexander the Great in 332 BC. Its great museum and library attracted the world's finest scholars and scientists. The works of Alexander the Great's tutor, the Greek scientist and philosopher Aristotle (384–322 BC), were also preserved there. His ideas on the universe and the natural world were to influence scholars for the next 2000 years, as were his ideas on women. A man of his times, Aristotle believed women to be inferior to men – and his views led to a general acceptance that science was a male preserve.

It was at Alexandria too that the medieval science of alchemy developed. Alchemists were looking for a way to change the form of metals, and in particular to turn common metals into silver and gold. These 'scientists' combined their theories with experiments, and were the founders of experimental chemistry. Alchemy had its roots partly in ancient Egypt, where production of cosmetics and perfume had been chemical industries supervised by women. Centuries later, women were still playing an important part in alchemy (an early name for the art was *opus mulierum*, or women's work). To the basic kitchen utensils employed for their experiments, alchemists introduced many pieces of apparatus familiar in today's science laboratories. Maria the Jewess, a renowned Alexandrian alchemist, is credited with devising apparatus essential to the development of laboratory chemistry.

Another Alexandrian scholar was the mathematician Hypatia, born in AD 370. Her scientist father had, unusually, educated her well. She taught at the Alexandrian schools, specializing in algebra and mechanics, and for her experiments she developed apparatus to distil water and to determine specific gravity in a liquid.

Scientific study was generally less important to the Romans,

> *Femaleness should be considered a deformity, though one which occurs in the ordinary course of nature.*
> Aristotle (384–322 BC)

Below *Hypatia, best known woman scientist of antiquity, is remembered mainly because of her horrific death in AD 415 when she was torn apart by a Christian mob.*

HILDEGARDIS *a Virgin Prophetess, Abbess of St Ruperts Nunnerye. She died at Bingen Aᵒ Do 1180 Aged 82 yeares.* *ill fec*

Abbess Hildegard of Bingen was the leading female monastic scholar of the Middle Ages. Her scientific writings show a quality of observation rare for the twelfth century. She was also an accomplished composer of music.

❛ ▬▬▬▬▬▬▬▬▬
Take them (women) from their housewifery and they are good for nothing! Martin Luther (1483–1546)
▬▬▬▬▬▬▬▬▬ ❜

who concentrated on practical subjects such as medicine and engineering. The old Greek theories were kept alive in Arab writings, and passed to Western Europe in the late Middle Ages. When Roman rule collapsed in western Europe around AD 500, scholars found refuge in monasteries; here lay a rare opportunity for women to pursue science. Many female monastic scholars enjoyed great independence, including the remarkable Abbess Hildegard of Bingen (1098–1179). Hildegard wrote knowledgeably and imaginatively on medicine, the origin of the universe, and many other aspects of medieval science.

Although women had never lost their domestic role as healers to the sick, in many societies they were restricted professionally to midwifery or folk medicine. But in Ancient Greece and Rome, educated noblewomen had studied medicine scientifically, and had run hospitals. Christian women, particularly in convents, also cared for the sick – continuing the tradition of trained female physicians and surgeons that goes back to ancient Egypt. The first medical school of medieval Europe was founded at Salerno, Italy, in the eleventh century and accepted both female students and teachers. It produced an eminent author of medical texts called Trotula. Some modern historians, doubting that a woman in the eleventh century could write a scholarly treatise, attributed her work to a man! Others decided that the 'Ladies of Salerno' were nurses and midwives, not physicians and teachers. But Italian historians claim that Trotula was a female scholar, whose works remained standard medical texts until the sixteenth century.

Italian universities were the only ones in Europe open to women, so as medicine became a profession requiring university education, it passed into the hands of men. Women still trained to become apothecaries and surgeons, but university-trained doctors wanted no competition from women healers practising folk medicine. These were increasingly branded as charlatans or witches.

After the monasteries were closed in England during the sixteenth century, women scholars lost their opportunities for study. Only in wealthy, aristocratic, or learned families could girls hope to be educated to the same degree as boys. Nor did many women have the independent financial means to support scientific study. But despite such handicaps, many wives, daughters and sisters of the new men of science throughout Europe collaborated with their male relatives. Sofie Brahe, for example, helped her astronomer brother Tycho to predict a lunar eclipse in 1573.

Women, denied access to academic education, were forced to remain onlookers to the scientific revolution, as scholars following the example of Copernicus sought scientific truth from their own observations. Discoveries came thick and fast. Science was

executed at *Chelmef-forde*, in the Countye of
Effex, *the 5. day of Iulye, laft paft.*
1 5 8 9.
¶ With the manner of their diuelifh practices and keeping of their
fpirits, whofe fourmes are heerein truelye
proportioned.

Left *Many 'wise women' who knew the secrets of herbal healing were condemned as witches and hung. These three women were executed at Chelsmford in Essex on 5 July 1589. The animals known as their 'familiars,' who were supposed to have been given to the witches by the Devil to act on his behalf, can be seen beneath the scaffold.*

fashionable in the seventeenth century, and educated gentlemen took to it as a hobby, starting new clubs and societies where they could talk about the latest developments. Founded in London in 1662, the Royal Society – like the universities – excluded women from membership.

Several of the leading seventeenth-century scientists were lent support by influential women. Queen Christina of Sweden encouraged the French mathematician René Descartes, and the Electress Sophia of Hanover gave aid to the German scientist Gottfried

Margaret Cavendish, Duchess of Newcastle (1623–73), was made fun of for her passion for science. But this 'scientific lady' stimulated other women's interest in popular science.

❛

I was mightily pleased, the other day, to find them all busy in preserving several fruits of the season . . . reading over **The Plurality of Worlds**. *It was very entertaining to me to see them dividing their speculations between jellies and stars, and making a sudden transition from the sun to an apricot.* Joseph Addison, *The Guardian* 8 September 1713

❜

von Leibniz. Elizabeth of Bohemia studied and lectured on Descartes, while her young cousins in London took lessons from Bathsua Makin, the first Englishwoman to advocate science teaching for girls.

Leibniz acknowledged his debt to the ideas of an English scholar, Lady Anne Conway (1631–79), who shared the fate of many female scholars when her theories were attributed to the man who published them.

Despite the fact that serious study was still considered unsuitable for women, an amateur interest in science became socially desirable in the seventeenth century. Manufacturers of microscopes and telescopes promoted these new inventions as curiosities for society ladies. Popular versions of scientific texts were written specifically for women readers.

In *Conversations on the Plurality of Worlds* (1686), the French author Bernard de Fontenelle hit on a popularizing format for scientific books which soon had them rivalling novels as favourite reading matter among ladies. He presented Descartes' ideas as a discussion between a teacher and his pupil, a 'lady of quality'. 'Simplifying' science for women by such methods may seem patronizing today, but such books as *Newtonianism for the Ladies* did keep an ever-growing female audience up to date with scientific knowledge, preparing the way for women to play an active part in science in the nineteenth century. Fontenelle's book was translated into English by the playwright and novelist Aphra Behn (1640–89), who criticized the author for making his female pupil say 'silly things', and for his interpretation of Descartes' theories.

French philosophers of the Enlightenment movement – Voltaire, Rousseau and Diderot – approved of popular science, though not of female education. Despite this, French women hosted salons for the leading intellectuals of the day. Marie Lavoisier (1758–1836) made her home a meeting place for scientists, while sharing in the chemical research of her husband Antoine.

In England, female intellectuals were mockingly named Bluestockings (after the hose worn by a male visitor to their gatherings). They included Elizabeth Carter (1717–1806), who translated from Italian a 'teacher and pupil' version of Isaac Newton's theories on optics. Another outstanding individual was Lady Mary Wortley Montagu (1689–1762), who introduced inoculation against smallpox into England.

By the end of the eighteenth century, science was expanding and dividing into various disciplines. Scientific books and periodicals were being published for women readers. Women were attending scientific lectures. The stage was set for women to re-enter the scientific scene.

Bathsua Makin (active 1641–73)

Bathsua Makin was one of the earliest authorities on women's education in England. She put forward the novel idea that schooling in the arts and sciences could be as valuable to women as to men.

Bathsua too was well educated, in science and mathematics as well as ancient and modern languages. She soon had a reputation as the most learned woman in the kingdom, and around 1641 was given the job of tutor to the children of Charles I.

She seems to have had a free hand to follow her own ideas on education, especially with the Princess Elizabeth, her best pupil. By the age of nine the Princess was proficient in Greek, Latin, Hebrew, French, Italian, Spanish – and mathematics. Although in 1650 Princess Elizabeth died, by then Bathsua had other distinguished female pupils, and may already have opened 'a school for gentlewomen' in Putney.

In 1673, Bathsua Makin set up a new school at Tottenham High Cross. Her pupils spent half their time in studying subjects taught at other schools for girls (such as dancing, music, religion, writing, accountancy); the rest of the curriculum consisted of Latin and French, history and geography, and scientific subjects, including natural history, astronomy and arithmetic. Students could choose to take additional courses as they wished – art, further languages, even philosophy.

Perhaps expecting opposition to her plans, Bathsua wrote *Essay to Revive the antient Education of Gentlewomen*, which included a list of women famous for their academic achievement, showing how they had succeeded as well as male scholars. She argued that women with the ability, means and time to undertake

Bathsua Making, royal tutor and a renowned scholar, was one of the first to propose a scheme of serious study for girls in the sciences as well as the arts.

such studies ought to have the opportunity to do so.

Answering the usual objections to 'serious' study for women, she outlined the advantages of giving them a good, overall education – noting not only the effect it would have on their families, but also the pleasure women themselves would gain from improving their minds. It is to Bathsua Makin that British women owe the introduction of science teaching in their schools.

Margaret Bryan, born about 1760, ran a boarding school for girls in Blackheath, London. Following the ideas of Erasmus Darwin, she included mathematics and science in the curriculum. She also published lectures on scientific subjects.

'

The leisure of the higher female classes is so great, and their influence in society so strong, that it is almost a duty that they should endeavour to awaken and keep alive a love of improvement and instruction. Let them make it disgraceful for men to be ignorant and ignorance will vanish.
Sir Humphry Davy (1778–1829)

'

2

The Natural Scientists

1800–1860

Eighteenth-century thinkers had expected scientific advance to change and improve society, and although the Industrial Revolution owed more to practical engineers than theoretical scientists, it did bring about social change during the nineteenth century. Machines began to replace manual labour; new jobs were created; women began to work outside the home. Just how many of the technical advances made during the Industrial Revolution were the result of women's ideas as they worked at spinning wheel or machine loom will never be known.

Science generally was still carried out by men – private individuals or trained professionals such as doctors and engineers. Women remained on the fringes, acting chiefly as observers and popularizers of the subject.

Even boys' schools rarely taught science, and it was a subject considered wholly unnecessary for females. Mary Wollstonecraft, Hannah More and Maria Edgeworth had campaigned for wider access to all-round education for women, and Erasmus Darwin (1731–1802), grandfather of the biologist Charles Darwin, advocated science teaching for girls. But only two schools, both in London, followed his suggestion.

In 1799, the Royal Institution opened in Albermarle Street, London, to promote scientific research. Dependent on subscriptions from both sexes, it invited fashionable women, as well as men, to attend its lectures. When the enthusiastic young scientist Humphry Davy was speaking, women flocked there in droves.

Among his audience was Jane Marcet (1769–1858), who, encouraged by her husband, became Davy's student and wrote a series of popular science books beginning with *Conversations on Chemistry, intended more especially for the Female Sex* (1806). It was first published anonymously (as was customary for women writers of Jane Marcet's social status) and the author was generally thought to be a man. The book stimulated interest in science among many readers, including the young Michael Faraday, who was to become one of the greatest scientists of all time.

Women writers continued to educate their women readers by

popularizing science. Natural history, a hobby for many country gentlemen and ladies in the eighteenth century, was still mainly a matter of collecting specimens, but the rage for rock and fossil-hunting made geology the leading science during the early years of the nineteenth century.

Among the first English fossil collectors were three sisters from Lyme Regis, Dorset – Mary, Margaret and Elizabeth Philpot – who supplied specimens to many early geologists. Their more famous friend Mary Anning (1799–1847) was actually able to support her family from sales of 'finds'. In 1821 the fossil skeleton of a prehistoric sea creature (a plesiosaur) brought her £200. The practical skills of recognizing and excavating fossil bones were matched by women's academic work, and in 1823 the Geological Society of London published the first scholarly paper by a woman (Marta Graham).

Other women geologists include Mary Morland (d.1857), who, with her husband William Buckland, identified and reconstructed the fossils they found on joint expeditions. She also edited and illustrated his books. Mary Horner (1808–73), an expert on mollusc

Thomas Rowlandson's satirical view of the fashionable audience for Humphry Davy's lectures at the Royal Institution. Enough women were attracted by the handsome and entertaining young chemist to draw mockery of 'scientific ladies'.

Fossil collectors such as Mary Anning helped to further the sciences of geology and palaeontology. Without formal training, she could predict where fossil remains might be found and developed the delicate skill of removing them from the surrounding rock.

6 ━━━━━━━━━━━━━

Botany has lately become a fashionable amusement with the ladies. But how the study of the sexual system of plants can accord with female modesty, I am not able to comprehend. I have, several times, seen boys and girls botanizing together. Rev Richard Polwhele, 1798

━━━━━━━━━━━━━ **9**

shells, joined her husband, Charles Lyell, in his geological work. As often happened, the independent research of both women was incorporated into that of their husbands.

Lyell gave geology lectures that were extremely popular with women, but the Bishop of London banned women from the audiences at King's College. Certain sciences were considered too taxing for female minds and bodies, so that ladies with scientific leanings were directed towards botany, although even this subject was thought to be unsuitable by some members of the church.

Perhaps not surprisingly, the Botanical Society of London, founded in 1836, was the first scientific society actively to encourage women members. Even in a 'female' subject, however, scholarly work was likely to be associated with male authorship. In 1840 Margaretta Riley (1804–99) submitted an essay on ferns to the Society. It was wrongly reported as being by her husband, who gained election to several scientific bodies as a result!

One subject rarely neglected in girls' education was drawing, and women excelled at botanical illustration. Keen observation and accurate drawing were essential to record new specimens for scientific study in the days before colour photography. Some of the best plant artists became fine botanists in their own right.

Among the foremost plant experts of her time was Anna Russell (1807–76). Known especially for her plant and fungi illustrations, she also published articles in scientific journals. Anne Pratt (1806–93), for some years an invalid, sketched plants collected by her sister for her five-volume *Flowering Plants and Ferns of Great Britain* (1855). She followed Priscilla Wakefield (1751–1832), author of *Introduction to Botany*, in the tradition of women botanical writers.

Natural history scholars too worked with their husbands. Sarah Lee accompanied her husband, Thomas Bowdich, to Africa, and to study the collections of the French zoologist Baron Cuvier. Later she wrote and illustrated popular books on natural science. The writings of Jane Webb (1807–58) were much admired by the gardening expert John Loudon (who thought them the work of a man). The two met and married, after which Jane Loudon's popular books on horticulture financed her husband's more 'scholarly' – and expensive – studies.

In this way, women observed and popularized science, while showing their potential as serious students. Some women published in the scientific journals. Some could now join a few of the institutions established to develop scientific activity – although women were still barred from the universities, where science was beginning to be taught and researched. In general, the tradition of the amateur scientist lasted longer in Britain than elsewhere in Europe, and several outstanding women contributed to it.

3

The Last Amateurs

1780–1870

In the early nineteenth century, there was little useful scientific training at British universities, and few posts existed for research scientists. Mathematics was an established subject, as were astronomy, mechanics and optics (thanks to Isaac Newton), but physics and chemistry were in their infancy and life sciences still mainly involved collecting specimens.

Women mathematicians had produced work of the first rank, despite their supposed 'weak' female intellect. For example, the Marquise du Châtelet (1706–49), had translated Newton's theories into French, proving herself a mathematician of genius. Another Frenchwoman, Sophie Germain (1776–1831), helped to found mathematical physics, and the Italian Maria Agnesi (1718–99), professor of mathematics at Bologna university, contributed to the development of calculus. Agnesi had encouragement from her

Keen amateur interest in astronomy and natural history paved the way for women's contribution to creative and theoretical scientific work.

Above *The brilliant Italian mathematician Maria Agnesi convinced many that women were capable of abstract thought.* **Right** *Madame du Châtelet, the French mathematician and physicist.*

> *I was present one day when she divided nine figures by nine other figures, entirely in her head . . . an astonished geometrician was there who could not follow what she did.*
> Voltaire (1694–1778) on the Marquise du Châtelet

mathematician father. Most women scholars still relied on male relatives for support, and male scholars in turn often used females in their families as assistants.

Caroline Herschel (1750–1848), born in Germany, came to join her musician brother William in England in 1772, as his housekeeper. But William, whose interest in astronomy had become a full-time occupation, needed her more and more to assist with his work. She ground lenses for telescopes, helped with his paperwork and, almost in spite of herself, grew fascinated by the stars. From 1782 she began observing the skies herself, with a telescope

> *I did nothing for my brother but what a well-trained puppy-dog would have done; that is to say, I did what he commanded me. I was a mere tool which he had the trouble of sharpening.* Caroline Herschel, 1876

Right *Caroline Herschel, educated in mathematics and astronomy by her brother William, kept his records and made calculations for him. Although later recognized as an astronomer in her own right, she saw her achievements only in terms of assisting her brother.*

William made for her. The following year she discovered three new nebulae.

Soon William became court astronomer, with Caroline recognized as his official paid assistant. She learned geometry and logarithms in order to make accurate calculations; she reorganized star catalogues to make William more efficient; she prepared his papers for publication. Recognized as the first woman to discover a comet, in 1786, she had recorded seven more by 1797, five of which were without doubt her discoveries. Between them, the Herschels extended the study of astronomy from the solar system to the stars.

Honoured publicly, Caroline disclaimed credit for her work, fearing it would lessen the reputation of her brother. Although fellow scientists recognized her as an important astronomer in her own right, Caroline found it difficult to see herself as anything more than an assistant.

Similarly self-taught was the second leading female scientist in Britain during the early nineteenth century, the respected mathematician Mary Somerville (1780–1872), whose career clearly shows the obstacles women faced to gain the education they needed. Her family was firmly against more than the minimum of education for a girl, but Mary enlisted an uncle's help to learn Latin and taught herself natural history. She became aware of algebra after seeing a puzzle in a women's magazine, and gained further gleanings in mathematics from overhearing her brother's lessons while she sat in the same room sewing.

In 1804, Mary married. Her husband had no interest in science and a low opinion of intellectual women. But his death three years later left her financially independent and free to concentrate on mathematics and astronomy, to the scorn of friends and family. Such reactions were typical of their time where women of obvious intelligence were concerned. Clever women tried to hide their gifts, since public display of female intellect did not fit a social climate in which genteel women were supposed to be protected by men. Above all, ladies must not betray their femininity by competing with males; that was bad manners and against the accepted laws of decency.

Fortunately, Mary's second husband, an army surgeon named William Somerville, was of a different mind. Encouraged by him to study subjects systematically, she took up Greek, botany, geology and mineralogy, moving on to astronomy, higher mathematics and physics. Now living in London, Mary moved in scientific circles, gaining in confidence and knowledge. In 1826 she presented a paper to the Royal Society describing her experiments in solar magnetism.

Despite a busy domestic and social life, Mary Somerville studied and wrote works which earned the respect of all the leading scientists of her time.

6 ▬▬▬▬▬▬▬▬▬▬

A man can always command his time under the plea of business; a woman is not allowed any such excuse . . . I was sometimes annoyed when in the midst of a difficult problem someone would enter and say, 'I have come to spend a few hours with you'. Mary Somerville (1780–1872)

▬▬▬▬▬▬▬▬▬▬▬▬▬ 9

Because mathematics in Britain lagged behind the rest of Europe at this time, Mary was asked to provide English versions of foreign works. Finding time from her responsibilities as mother and housekeeper she produced a version of *The Mechanisms of the Heavens* (1831) by the French scientist Laplace. The book put Mary Somerville at the forefront of scientific writing (and caused her to be called 'a godless woman' in the House of Commons!). Other books by Mary Somerville, *On the Connexion of the Physical Sciences* (1834) and *Physical Geography* (1848), were as highly acclaimed. A sentence in *Physical Sciences* spurred the astronomer John Couch Adams to look for (and find) the planet Neptune.

Mary sadly attributed her own lack of scientific discoveries to a deficiency of the female sex. In fact, she had lost her most creative years through lack of tuition and opportunity. Like her acquaintance, the mathematician Ada Lovelace, Mary accepted the view that study weakened a woman's health, blaming herself for her daughter's death because she encouraged the girl to work hard. The brilliant nineteenth-century female mathematicians were regarded by contemporaries of both sexes as freaks, not as serious students requiring tuition and guidance. They made their way as best they could, and their achievements are therefore all the more remarkable.

The Royal Society placed a bust of Mary Somerville in its hall, an honour given in place of actual membership. She was among the last great amateur scientists. At the end of her long life, science had become too complex, its branches too specialized, to be mastered in its entirety by one person. From now on, scientists would concentrate on certain areas. Women were to move gradually from data-collecting and summarizing to taking a full part in experimental and creative work.

> *The very great tension of mind which they (mathematical studies) require is beyond the strength of women's physical power of application.* Professor De Morgan to Lady Byron, 1844

> *Had our friend Mrs Somerville been married to Laplace, or some mathematician, we should never have heard of her work. She would have merged it in her husband's and passed it off as his.* Charles Lyell, 1831

Right *Denied entry to the Royal Society because of her sex, Mary Somerville was instead honoured by having a bust of her placed in its Great Hall. An outspoken feminist, she was the first to sign John Stuart Mill's petition for women's suffrage (1867).*

MARY SOMERVILLE

Ada, Countess of Lovelace (1815–52)

Ada was the daughter of Anne Isabella Milbanke, an heiress and mathematician, and of Lord Byron, the poet. Five weeks after Ada's birth, her parents parted. Realizing that the girl was gifted, her mother employed good tutors, including William Frend, a Cambridge academic who had taught Lady Byron algebra, geometry and astronomy.

Ada was often ill, suffering from migraines, but by fourteen, she had mastered mathematics, astronomy, music and Latin. Her ambition was to be a famous scientist.

In 1834, she attended some lectures on the work of the mathematician Charles Babbage (1792–1871). Knowing that the mathematical calculating tables of the day were full of errors, Babbage was sure there must be a mechanical way to work them out accurately. For the rest of his life he designed calculating machines.

Intrigued, Ada began studying Babbage's work. Her sympathetic husband, William King, Earl of Lovelace, joined the Royal Society to copy out extracts from books and papers for her. In 1842, a description of Babbage's 'analytical engine' (forerunner of the modern computer) was published in French. Ada translated it and, as Babbage suggested, made additional notes.

Ada's 'notes' (three times as long as the original description) prove how well she understood the way a computer might work. She described how the machine could be programmed, and devised several advanced mathematical programs of her own. She also predicted future uses for the machine, such as the composing of music.

To build his computer, Babbage needed a

Ada Lovelace enjoyed mathematics, but although brilliant and perceptive, her genius lacked systematic training.

great deal of money. In fact the machine was too advanced for existing engineering materials and techniques. But Ada persuaded Babbage and her husband that she had a 'foolproof' system for backing racehorses. The system failed, Ada fell heavily into debt, secretly pawned the family jewels, and became the victim of blackmail. She was also ill.

Complaining that 'too much mathematics' had caused her problems, Ada Lovelace died at the age of thirty-six. A brilliant mathematician, she had, as a woman, been denied the university education which could have directed her talents more usefully.

4

Practical Work

1870–1900

Marianne North was the most famous of the 19th-century women botanical artists.
Above *Painting in South Africa.*
Below *Intrepidly sketching before an audience in Egypt, 1868.*

As Britain became the industrial leader and 'workshop of the world' in the nineteenth century, science moved into partnership with new technologies. Scientific developments were radically changing people's lives and beliefs. The self-supporting 'amateur' was steadily giving way to professional scientists and technologists. Women were not among their number, either in universities or factories (except as unskilled labour).

Generally, men and women were still seen to belong to different 'natural' spheres, although it was acknowledged that women could achieve much – in their own 'feminine' fields of study. There was Marianne North (1830–90), for example, the most famous of the nineteenth-century women botanists.

Marianne North had enjoyed visits to the Royal Botanical Gardens at Kew, where she studied and drew plants. She also travelled with her parents in Europe and the Middle East, making

sketches to record what she saw. When her father died in 1869, she was determined to paint plants in their natural surroundings, and so she did – in Jamaica, North and South America, Japan, India, Australia, South Africa and the Seychelles. In the process she discovered four previously unknown plants (which were named after her) and introduced many more species into Europe. To display her paintings, she had a gallery built at Kew, and an admiring Queen Victoria regretted there was no feminine version of a knighthood with which to honour her.

Marianne North was single, with enough money after her father's death to support her travels. Her married sister Catherine, also a painter of flowers, lacked Marianne's freedom to pursue her interest independently. Her works remain largely unknown.

Margaret Gatty extended botanical study to marine biology, publishing *British Seaweeds* in 1863. (It included a section on suitable clothing for women collectors!) The tendency to specialize, and the movement towards 'professionalism', was demonstrated by Eleanor Ormerod, who singlehandedly created a science and a profession – that of economic entomologist.

Women's exclusion from university education and the obtaining of university degrees, had been the main stumbling block to their full participation in science. But in the nineteenth century campaigns for educational reform steadily grew.

In 1848 Queen's College, founded in London to educate young women planning to teach, gave them the opportunity to study

But let us consider, point by point, how the need to teach girls some science arises from the duties they will have to fulfil as wives, mothers and educators. Anguilli, 1876

Left *The North Gallery at London's Kew Gardens houses over 800 of Marianne North's botanical paintings. As with other women 'flower artists', her interest in accurate drawing made her an expert in botany. She introduced new plants to Europe and several species were named after her.*

Somerville College, Oxford University, founded in 1879 and named after the mathematician Mary Somerville, was one of the colleges women set up for themselves to take advantage of higher education.

mathematics. London University, founded in 1836, ruled in its charter that women be admitted to degree courses, but did not grant them degrees until 1878 – the first British university to do so. Women continued to apply to Oxford and Cambridge colleges, duly being allowed to sit the entrance examinations, but not being awarded places. Led by Emily Davies (1830–1921) and Anne Clough (1820–92), women eventually established their own residential colleges at these universities (including Somerville College, Oxford, founded in 1879 and named after Mary Somerville). However, it was not until 1922 that first degrees were awarded to women at Cambridge – and only in 1947 were these made 'real' degrees, identical to men's.

Eleanor Anne Ormerod (1828–1901)

Reading a *Manual of British Beetles* at the age of twenty-three started Eleanor Ormerod on a serious study of insects, and a career as an economic entomologist; that is, she studied how insects affect farming production, for good or ill. Not that she would have seen her work as a 'career'. For all her expert knowledge, she remained an amateur scientist. Her painstakingly compiled reports, all fully illustrated, were printed at her own expense, and sent free to any interested correspondents throughout the world.

Born in Gloucestershire, Eleanor was the youngest of ten children and, as customary for the time, learned elementary subjects at home with her mother, but she also taught herself Latin and modern languages. Like many other girls, she was encouraged to take an interest in natural history, and especially in plants.

In 1868 Eleanor helped the Royal Horticultural Society to mount an exhibition of 'insects beneficial or injurious to Man'. In 1872 she sent models of insects 'injurious' to plants to an exhibition in Moscow. When, in 1873, her father died and the Ormerod home broke up, Eleanor and Georgiana settled for a time in a house near to Kew Gardens. Here Eleanor recorded weather observations, for which, in 1878, she was elected first woman fellow of the Meteorological Society. But her main interest remained insects and how to eradicate insect pests.

Eleanor Ormerod, whose hobby of studying insects led to worldwide improvements in agriculture and the founding of a new science – economic entomology.

Eleanor Ormerod started her 'Annual reports of Observations of Injurious Insects' in 1877, gathering notes from observers all over the world. Governments and farming and horticultural bodies all received her advice for free. She waged war most successfully against the ox-warble fly, but tackled with equal vigour insect pests of farm, forest, garden and orchard.

She was consultant to the Royal Agricultural Society of England (1882–92) and special lecturer to the Royal Agricultural College (1881–84). Agricultural societies throughout the world honoured her for helping farmers to improve their crop yields and keep their stock healthy. Thus her socially acceptable interest in natural history led Eleanor Ormerod, self-taught insect expert, to help feed the growing population of the modern world.

Eleanor A. Ormerod

5

Medical Matters

1850–1880

This nineteenth century cartoon portrays a patient only too pleased to have the attentions of a female physician! It illustrates the difficulty that women sometimes experienced in being taken seriously as doctors.

Women had been barred from the medical profession in England since the late Middle Ages. The female surgeons and apothecaries who once practised their skills had vanished as medicine was taken over by professional physicians with medical degrees. Only men could gain such qualifications, and so only men could become doctors.

Women healers still existed, of course, dispensing traditional advice and home-made cures. Seventeenth-century ladies experimented with herbs and chemical remedies, particularly Mary Boyle and Katherine Jones, sisters of the chemist Robert Boyle. And there were always the midwives.

During the seventeenth and eighteenth centuries, several women had tried to raise the standards of midwifery – notably Jane Sharp, Hester Shaw, Elizabeth Cellier and Sarah Stone – and to fight the attempt by male midwives to take over their work. Sarah Stone argued that it was not improper for women to read anatomy books and see dissections, as she had done. But despite

> *It is impossible that a woman whose hands reek with gore can be possessed of the same nature or feeling as the generality of women.*
> Newspaper columnist on Elizabeth Blackwell, 1859

Right *A midwife delivers a baby into a wealthy 17th-century family. Midwifery remained the one area in which women could practise medical skills, even when entry to the medical profession was denied them.*

their efforts, such 'man midwives' as the Chamberlens (a family who invented and kept secret a type of forceps used in childbirth) nearly succeeded in removing women from their last traditional healing role.

A few women, generally classed as 'quacks', were spectacularly successful in inventing 'secret' remedies; Joanna Stephens (d.1774), for example, found a way of dissolving bladder stones and claimed to have cured Sir Robert Walpole, Britain's first prime minister.

Their humble place in the medical world ensured that midwives and 'professional' nurses were held in low esteem in the nineteenth century. Such was the situation when Florence Nightingale revolutionized nursing and public health, opening her School for Nurses at St Thomas's Hospital in London in 1860. By making nursing a respectable profession for women of every class, she had a profound effect on the position of women in society.

And yet women still could not take a medical degree to qualify as doctors. The amazing history of Dr Barry (1795–1865) echoes centuries-old stories of women disguising themselves as men to study medicine. In 1812, Miranda Barry graduated from Edinburgh School of Medicine as James Barry and began a most successful career as army surgeon, being appointed Inspector-General of Canadian Hospitals in 1857. The deception was revealed at her death, although the authorities still insisted that Dr Barry had been male. Others labelled her hermaphrodite.

The disguise ruse was suggested by one college professor to Elizabeth Blackwell (1821–1910) when she declared a desire to

> *Young ladies all, of every clime,*
> *Especially of Britain,*
> *Who wholly occupy your time*
> *In novels or in knitting,*
> *Whose highest skill is but to play,*
> *Sing, dance, or French to clack well,*
> *Reflect on the example, pray,*
> *Of excellent Miss Blackwell!*
>
> Punch

Above *James Barry – the name under which Miranda Barry graduated as a doctor from Edinburgh School of Medicine in 1812 – in Army uniform.*

Left *Elizabeth Blackwell, the first woman doctor of modern times, lectured in the USA and Europe to advance the cause of women in medicine and to encourage others to follow her example.*

take up medicine. Born in England, she had gone with her family to the USA in 1832 and graduated as the first woman doctor of modern times in 1849. But her entrance to college was by mere chance, when the male medical undergraduates voted for her to join their course partly as a joke.

Already well known in Britain from previous visits, in 1858 Elizabeth Blackwell returned to give a series of lectures. Regular members of her audience were Emily Davies (1830–1921), a determined champion for women's education, and her friend Elizabeth Garrett (1836–1917). Thinking Elizabeth an ideal pioneer, Emily Davies encouraged her to take on the medical establishment.

Although women could train as doctors in the USA or in Switzerland, such qualifications were unrecognized in Britain. The British medical profession demanded training at a British medical school and the passing of British examinations.

An introduction to a director of the Middlesex Hospital gave Elizabeth her chance. She became an unofficial medical student there in 1860 (and did so well that male students demanded her removal). But in 1865, having finished the lecture course and

Below *Elizabeth Garrett gaining her medical qualification in Paris, where degrees in medicine were open to women.*

five-year apprenticeship demanded, she gained a diploma from the Society of Apothecaries – the only medical examining board with a charter that did not exclude women. (The Society then promptly changed its charter to prevent anyone following her example.) Elizabeth Garrett's name was added to the Medical Register, but still no British university would accept her to study for a degree.

As the University of Paris had allowed women on its degree course in 1868, she learned French to take her degree there in 1870. The British Medical Register refused to recognize her qualification but, with the support of her husband, James Anderson, she began work as a surgeon. She founded a clinic for women and gradually gained acceptance from the medical community.

Elizabeth Garrett had succeeded as an individual, but the route she had followed was now barred to others until a remarkable struggle by a group of women, headed by Sophia Jex-Blake (1840–1912), finally won the battle.

Sophia Jex-Blake applied to study medicine at Edinburgh University in 1869, on the grounds that many women wanted treatment by doctors of their own sex. Despite opposition from several professors and physicians, she and four other female students managed to arrange their own classes, gaining special permission to attend lectures and examinations. (Women, when allowed to study at universities, were often denied use of facilities such as laboratories, while mixed lectures could take place only if the professor approved.) The Edinburgh women were so successful in their studies that some male students tried to stop them taking an anatomy examination by rioting outside the gates.

When the University steadfastly refused to award the women degrees, they took their case to court, but to no avail. Sophia Jex-Blake and her group became the centre of national controversy. Their case was strengthened by the fact that several women who had qualified abroad were already practising in England. In the end, Sophia Jex-Blake herself studied in Switzerland (which opened university education to women in 1854), returning to found the London School of Medicine for Women in 1874. She finally took her MD degree in Dublin, in 1877, after the Irish College of Physicians agreed to admit women to examinations on the same terms as men.

In January 1878 London University voted itself a new charter admitting women to all degrees and in 1882 Edith Shove and Mary Scharlieb became its first medical graduates. The 'unladylike' fight by Sophia Jex-Blake had made the medical battle headline news and finally won the day.

Armed with university qualifications, women could begin to take a full part not only in medical life, but in all areas of science.

Sophia Jex-Blake, who spearheaded the struggle to make medicine a career open to all women in Britain.

❛

Let it remain; it has more sense than those who sent it here. Dr Handyside, when a sheep was pushed into the room where Sophia Jex-Blake and other women medical students were taking examinations

❜

Mary Ann Dacomb Scharlieb (1844–1930)

Mary Bird was born in London into a merchant's family. She married William Scharlieb, a barrister, in 1865, sailed with him to India (then under British rule) and settled in Madras. The practice of purdah in many Indian families made her realize how much her new country needed qualified medical women.

Purdah (literally meaning 'a curtain', for screening off women's apartments from public view) decreed that women in strict religious families rarely met men other than close relatives. To give vaccinations in households where male doctors were not admitted, the medical authorities in Madras trained a few women. So useful were they, that a scheme for training midwives in the same way was proposed. The state government was urged to allow women into the Madras Medical College, and in 1874 three women, including Mary Scharlieb, applied for admission.

> *If it be unwomanly for a woman to study medicine with a man, how much more must it be so for her to be medically examined by a man when she is ill?* Oxford Undergraduates' Journal 1870

In 1878 Dr Mary Scharlieb returned to England, where the battle for women to gain medical qualifications still raged. Entering the London School of Medicine for Women, she and Edith Shove became the first two women medical graduates of London in 1882.

The following year, she went back to Madras to found a small hospital for Hindu

Mary Scharlieb realized that some women would accept medical care only from other women and that many more would prefer doctors of their own sex.

and Muslim women, returning to London in 1887 to work at the New Hospital (later the Elizabeth Garrett Anderson Hospital).

Mary Scharlieb was the first woman to gain the MD of London University, the first woman to become consultant to a general teaching hospital (the Royal Free in London), and in 1920 she became one of the first six women magistrates. In 1926 she was created a Dame.

Pioneers in Britain, notably Sophia Jex-Blake, could cite Mary Scharlieb (and other women who had qualified in medicine outside Britain) in their own battle for recognition as doctors. They also knew that the preference of Indian women for doctors of their own sex was shared by many in Britain. Those who shied from consulting male physicians might visit a woman more readily. Mary Scharlieb, who had seen this need so clearly, provided a distinguished example for medical women of both countries.

6

Power Sharing

1900–1935

Scientific work in the nineteenth century had laid the foundations of a second industrial revolution. In the twentieth century, transport and communications, for example, were revolutionized by the motor car, the aeroplane, and wireless telegraphy. Technological developments were to change women's lives as radically. The typewriter, invented in the 1870s, created a new kind of 'respectable' work for women; household equipment such as the vacuum cleaner and washing machine aided – then replaced – domestic servants. But it was the First World War (1914–18) that hastened both technological advance and women's rights.

With an unprecedented number of men called up to fight, women were required to take their place in shops, offices and factories. They proved physically and mentally capable of doing 'men's' jobs; they drove tractors and buses; they operated heavy machinery; in munitions works their 'nimble fingers' were admired for their quick skill.

Above *An engineer checks the controls of a steam engine during the First World War, when women proved their ability to do heavy, 'unladylike' work. Many enjoyed learning and using technical skills, but few remained in engineering when men returned to claim their old jobs.*

Left *Members of the Women's Royal Naval Service (Wrens) testing radio valves at a Royal Navy signals school. Many women gained experience of technology during the First World War, in factories or in the newly formed women's services.*

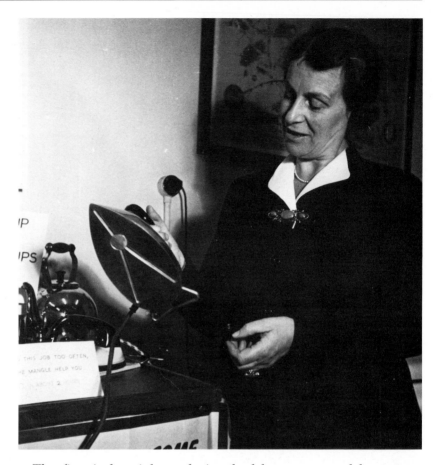

Right *Caroline Haslett examines an electric iron at an exhibition of household equipment, one of the means by which she tried to familiarize women with advances in technology.*

The first industrial revolution had been powered by steam; the second was generated by electricity. And as the first had introduced women to factory work, so the second made them familiar with the production line. Someone who experienced industrial methods and mechanization at first hand was Dame Caroline Haslett (1895–1957), who fought hard to bring women and technology together.

From childhood Caroline had preferred tinkering in her father's workshop to helping with cooking or housework. And her father, a railway engineer, had ensured that all his children learned to use tools properly. Enduring treatment for a weak spine, Caroline had to lie on her back for five hours a day, watching her mother do the housework: carrying in coals, cleaning and leading the stove, cleaning flues, washing, starching, ironing, scrubbing, polishing, dusting – all by hand. To Caroline it seemed such a terrible waste of time. If a man's working hours were limited by law, why not a woman's, she wondered.

She took a job in the office of an engineering company, drawing up quotations and specifications for the boilers the company made and sold. Soon she knew as much about boilers as anyone; she asked for a transfer to the works where, during the First World War, her engineering skill and knowledge developed rapidly. Similar experiences were shared by other women, but after the war, demobilized soldiers came back to claim their old jobs. Most of the women who had temporarily occupied them went back to their previous work, or went home, where they remained during the slump and unemployment of the 1920s and 1930s.

Caroline Haslett had found no difficulties in working alongside men, and had proved that women could succeed in a field which was almost exclusively male. At the age of twenty-four she became organizing secretary for the recently founded Women's Engineering Society (WES), which aimed to promote the study and practice of engineering among women. Caroline saw it as an opportunity to reinforce the inroads into engineering made by

'

I expect you have come about typing, but I have to see a fellow about some boilers first. To Caroline Haslett, the 'fellow' expected

'

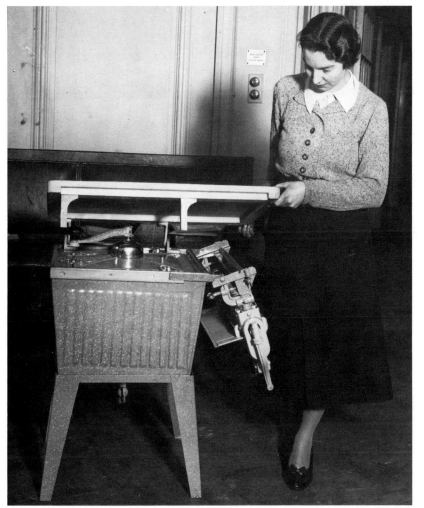

'

Look at this square kettle and saucepan; they're the invention of a woman. You can put four of them together over one hotplate – at a considerable saving in power. Caroline Haslett, on gadgets in her flat, to a reporter writing an article on "Miss All-alone at Home", 1925

'

Left *This award-winning, all-in-one washer and ironing board, designed by Mrs Peace of Sheffield, was featured in an exhibition of inventions in London in 1938. Such practical labour-saving devices are typical of inventions made by women.*

women during the war. She worked to break down employers' prejudice against female labour, and to persuade the engineering institutions to allow women to take professional qualifications.

But her experience of industrial methods also made Caroline eager to apply them in the home, to ease household drudgery, and she wanted women to take an active part in harnessing technology for their own use. She saw electricity as the answer to women's captivity by housework, and in 1924 founded the Electrical Association for Women. It organized lectures, arranged visits to power stations and produced books and magazines all aimed at familiarizing women with electricity and electrical appliances. Through it, government heard women's views on wiring, apparatus, costs and methods of charging for electricity, education in schools and the training of women in the electrical industry. Caroline Haslett pleaded for housewives' opinions to be taken into account before domestic equipment was standardized. She saw clearly that the domestic development of electricity would come through women's involvement, and that it would be a social force to change everyone's lives.

Women's lives were also profoundly revolutionized by improved health care and by wider knowledge and practice of birth control. This was pioneered by Marie Stopes (1881–1958), whose clinics gave information which freed many women from the burden of over-large families. By such advances, science and technology increased women's independence.

Right *Marie Stopes, pioneer of birth control, studying a microscope slide. Herself a botanist, Dr Stopes's books were aimed at ordinary women readers. Wider practice of birth control improved women's health and their opportunity to pursue worthwhile careers.*

7

Taking the Field

1900–1950

Women chemists working with men in a laboratory at Leeds University, 1908. With access to higher education, many more women could begin to contribute to scientific theory and practice.

Theoretical science was also revolutionizing the world, with discoveries that changed people's views of the universe – much as Copernicus's had done centuries before. Marie Curie had discovered that radioactivity was a property of the atom, Einstein formed his theory of relativity (1905), and Niels Bohr, Max Planck, Einstein and Ernest Rutherford created modern nuclear physics. Science became so complex that professionals concentrated more on particular fields of expertise – and gained new names: molecular biologists, geneticists, astrophysicists.

Women were active in the new fields, but old prejudices lingered too. In 1907, when the Austrian physicist Lise Meitner (1878–1968) went to work in Germany, one professor made her promise never to enter laboratories where men were working! By the 1920s Meitner was herself professor of physics at the university of Berlin, and in 1939 she published – with her nephew – the first paper on nuclear fission.

Women physicists therefore made two of the potentially greatest scientific discoveries of the twentieth century: radium by Marie Curie and nuclear fission by Lise Meitner.

As in the past, women could only prove their ability when they were given the opportunity. Explaining why women – herself included – excelled at X-ray crystallography, Dame Kathleen Lonsdale credited William Bragg's encouraging leadership at the Royal Institution from 1923 onwards. The Institution's laboratories had been open to both sexes from their establishment in 1896, and William Bragg invited women as well as men to join his research team.

Another woman scientist, Dorothy Needham, looked back in the late 1970s over forty-five years of research to comment on her early experience: 'I simply existed on one research grant after another, devoid of position, rank or assured emolument [salary] . . . I belong to the generation for whom it was calmly assumed that married women would be supported financially by their husbands, and if they chose to work in the laboratory all day and half the night, it was their own concern.' In effect, although

❛

The female mind is incapable of grasping mechanics or high mathematics or any of the fundamentals taught in this course. College course adviser to Emily Hahn, 1926

❜

Above *In 1964 Dorothy Hodgkin became only the third woman to receive the Nobel Prize for Chemistry, in recognition of her work in X-ray crystallography.*

women could pursue research, a career aimed at a top university post – or any other – was hardly ever considered. One woman who realized the need for an independent teaching job was Dorothy Crowfoot Hodgkin (b. 1910), whose lifelong interest – X-ray crystallography – was aroused by reading William Bragg's *Concerning the Nature of Things* in 1925. Because of her enthusiasm for science, she was allowed, with another girl pupil, to join the boys at her school in doing chemistry. Later she studied at Somerville College, and began a career in research.

When a beam of X-rays is passed through a crystal, the rays make a pattern which is recorded on a photographic plate. The pattern shows how the atoms in the crystal are arranged, and so X-ray crystallography is used to find the atomic structure of various substances. It demands great patience and imagination. In 1933, Dorothy Hodgkin made the first X-ray photograph of a protein (pepsin).

During the Second World War (1939–45), there was an enormous demand for penicillin, the first antibiotic, and scientists strove to find ways of producing it in quantity. Dorothy Hodgkin established the chemical structure of penicillin, laying the foundation for future developments in producing the drug.

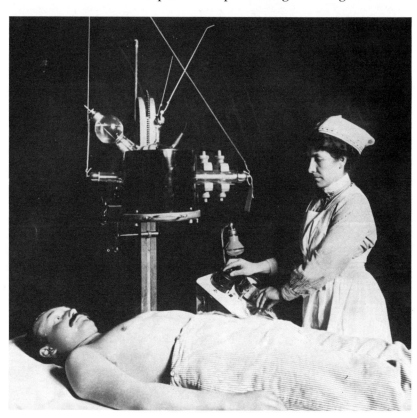

Right *A nurse uses one of the new X-ray machines at a German military hospital during the First World War.*

Left *Students in a science laboratory at Girton College for women at Cambridge University in 1930.*

After the war, in 1948, scientists were studying vitamin B_{12}, which builds red blood cells and protects the body against pernicious anaemia. Again, Dorothy Hodgkin found the vitamin's structure, this time with the help of one of the first electronic computers. Called 'the greatest triumph of crystallographic technique that has yet occurred', this work, together with that on penicillin, won her the Nobel Prize for Chemistry in 1964. She was only the third woman to be given the Chemistry award, following Marie Curie (1911) and her daughter Irène Joliot-Curie (1935).

Dorothy Hodgkin later studied the structure of insulin, but was hampered by the onset of arthritis in her hands. In 1965 she was awarded the Order of Merit – the only woman apart from Florence Nightingale ever to receive this honour. Speaking to Swedish students on behalf of the 1964 Nobel Prizewinners, she said, 'I was chosen to reply to you this evening as the one woman of our group, a position which I hope very much will not be so very uncommon in the future that it will call for any comment or distinction of this kind, as more and more women carry out research in the same way as men.'

'

A great many girls do not see the point of further education once they have got a job. Their hopes are naturally bent on marriage and they fear perhaps – though there is much experience to prove them wrong – that by aiming at a certificate they may miss a husband. Government report on technical education, 1956

'

Kathleen Lonsdale (1903–71)

Kathleen Lonsdale enjoyed referring to herself as an 'old lag'. A member of the Society of Friends (Quakers) and therefore a pacifist, she went to prison in 1943, during the Second World War, for refusing to register for Civil Defence. Two years later she became the first woman Fellow of the Royal Society.

A brilliant research scientist with a keen moral conscience, Kathleen Lonsdale's acute concern was that twentieth-century science should be wisely and humanely applied. Her scientific achievements were recognized by her election to the Royal Society, but she worked as energetically for world peace, prison reform, and an improved status for women in the scientific community.

She was born Kathleen Yardley, youngest child in a family of ten, on 28 January 1903 in Newbridge, Ireland. The family later moved to England, where Kathleen won a scholarship to Ilford County High School for Girls. In order to study physics, chemistry and higher mathematics, however, she had to take lessons at the local boys' school. At the early age of sixteen she started a degree course at Bedford College, London University, and headed the University BSc Honours list in 1922 with the highest marks awarded in ten years. One of the examiners, the Nobel-prize-winning physicist Sir William Bragg, asked her to join his research team.

She specialized in X-ray crystallography, studying atoms and molecules by examining the patterns made as an X-ray beam passes through a crystal. Kathleen Lonsdale took most pride in her proof that the carbon atoms in benzene are arranged in a hexagonal (six-sided) pattern. She also developed an X-ray technique to measure the distance between diamond atoms (Lonsdaleite, a diamond found in meteorites, was named after her), and applied crystallography to medical problems such as bladder stones.

She became professor of chemistry at University College, London, in 1949, was made a Dame in 1956, and was awarded the Davy Medal of the Royal Society in 1957. She also served as British President of the Women's International League for Peace and Freedom.

Believing that scientists should ensure that their work is used in the service of humankind, she campaigned tirelessly for this end, for her peace work, and to encourage other women to enter the scientific field.

Kathleen Lonsdale, first women Fellow of the Royal Society saw the need for scientific knowledge to be used in the service of humanity.

8

Lost Contributions

1950–1980s

By the late 1940s, women scientists were at work in universities, in industry and, perhaps most important of all, in schools teaching a younger generation. The Second World War had (like the First) given more women a taste of working outside the home, and introduced them to technical (though usually low-grade) jobs in factories.

Meanwhile women still excelled in their traditional scientific areas, as they do today. The 'collecting, cataloguing and recording' tradition of astronomy continued; that of geology expanded into anthropology and archaeology.

In Africa, Mary Leakey (b. 1913) worked alongside her husband Louis in Tanzania's Olduvai Gorge, tracing the evolution of humankind. It was Mary who discovered many of the important fossils which pushed back further and further the history of our ancestors' life on earth. Some of these finds were widely credited to her husband. The couple separated, but Mary continued her work in and around the Gorge, and in 1976 she found humanlike footprints made in volcanic ash some 3.5 million years ago. Her

A British Rail engineer. Women technologists are steadily moving into fields traditionally dominated by men.

Left *The anthropologist Mary Leakey, working in and around Olduvai Gorge in Tanzania, made discoveries of pre-human remains which demonstrated that human development began at least a million years earlier than had been thought.*

suggestion that upright walking had developed so far back in time challenged yet again all previous ideas on the time-scale of human development.

The archaeologist Kathleen Kenyon (1906–78) studied human history in the Middle East. From 1952 to 1958, she excavated the ancient city of Jericho, in Jordan. She was able to date the site back to 7000 BC (making Jericho the oldest known town in the world) and in so doing highlighted the significance of cities in the development of civilization.

Such scientists were following in the tradition of the nineteenth-century collectors and explorers – women like Marianne North, Isabella Bird Bishop (1831–1904), Mary Kingsley (1862–1900), and Amelia Edwards (1831–92), who was among the first to study the remains of ancient Egypt.

Among astronomers, Margaret Burbidge is notable for being the first woman Director of the Royal Greenwich Observatory, appointed in 1972. She acted as director of the London University Observatory (1950–51), but when, in 1955, her husband Geoffrey (a fellow astronomer) gained a Carnegie fellowship for research at California's famous Mount Wilson Observatory, she had to take a minor research job at the state's Institute of Technology. Women were not then eligible for an appointment such as her husband's.

Margaret Burbidge's particular interest were quasars, as well as studying how elements are formed deep inside stars through nuclear fusion. Her book *Quasi-Stellar* Objects (1967) was written in collaboration with her husband.

And so the familiar pattern of women scholars working alongside male relatives continues, perhaps not surprisingly in science, where collaboration and team work are so important, particularly in research. However, women scientists have also been subject to patronizing and sometimes hostile attitudes from male colleagues – most famously in the case of Rosalind Franklin (1921–58).

Rosalind Franklin was an X-ray crystallographer. She had begun her career by doing research into tiny three-dimensional forms in coal (carbon), working with structures so minute that the unit of measurement in one experiment, for example, was a single molecule of helium. At that time, the early 1940s, nobody dreamed it would be possible to discover the structure of the body's biological substances using similar methods.

But X-ray crystallography developed rapidly, and in 1951 Rosalind Franklin was invited to build up an X-ray unit in the biophysics department at King's College, London. One of the department's projects was to analyse the structure of DNA, the substance which carries the body's genetic code. Along with scientists elsewhere in Britain and abroad, they were trying to find

Margaret Burbidge, one of the world's leading astronomers, was appointed first woman director of the Royal Greenwich Observatory in 1972. She was not, however, honoured with the title of Astronomer Royal, traditionally given to holders of the post.

Left *Rosalind Franklin in France, where she worked on X-ray analysis of carbon. The techniques she developed there later helped to unravel the secrets of DNA, the genetic code controlling heredity.*

out how heredity works. When Rosalind worked at King's, scientific research there was male-dominated; there was only one other woman on the laboratory staff.

Another approach to the DNA problem was being made at Cambridge by Francis Crick and James Watson, who were building models of the DNA molecule to try and find its structure. Unknown to Rosalind, a copy of one of her papers, and her best photograph of a form of DNA, were shown to Watson in 1952 by her fellow researcher at King's, Maurice Wilkins. The photograph showed DNA to be in the form of a helix (a screw-shaped coil).

This information was crucial. Crick and Watson worked out a new model, and in 1953 the scientific magazine *Nature* published papers on DNA by Watson and Crick, by Wilkins and by Rosalind Franklin.

Unhappy at King's, Rosalind moved to another college to work on the polio virus and a virus of tobacco. In 1958 she died. In 1962, Watson, Crick and Wilkins were given the Nobel Prize for their work on the structure of DNA. Watson wrote a book about the discovery, *The Double Helix* (1968), which made patronizing and sexist references to Rosalind Franklin. A defence of the scientist, and another version of the events described by Watson, was published by Anne Sayre in *Rosalind Franklin and DNA* (1975). Both books reflect the problems, difficulties and frustrations faced by an able, intelligent woman in the scientific world of her time.

Part of the problem Rosalind Franklin met at King's College involved status. Although asked to set up her own operation in the biophysics laboratory, she was regarded by Maurice Wilkins as an assistant. Women had been accustomed to a supporting role for so long that they – and men likewise – often expected and accepted this. When, like Rosalind Franklin, they did not, friction could result.

The problem of self-image has had far-reaching effects on women's participation in science. In an address to the Royal Institution in 1970, Kathleen Lonsdale examined the causes for the relative dearth of women scientists. She pinpointed a lack of

Right *A research scientist working at Trinidad's Institute for Marine Affairs. In developing countries, the scientific contribution made by women is of special importance.*

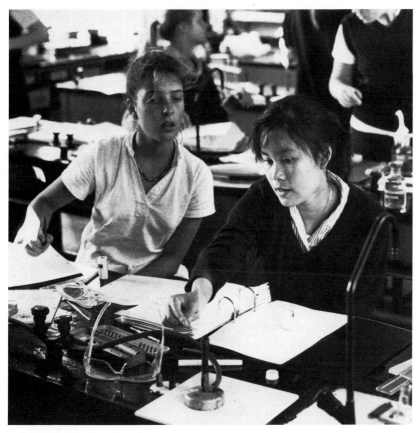

Left *Science students at a girls' school. Surveys show that encouragement from teachers – and parents – is vitally important in steering women towards scientific careers.*

women school teachers in scientific subjects, girls opting for 'general science' rather than mathematics, pure physics or chemistry, and more men than women choosing to continue research after graduating; she also noted the small percentage of women appointed to responsible or creative academic posts.

In her opinion, few women rose to top positions in science because of career-breaks for marriage and children. As a result there were few role models for girl students to follow and, knowing the difficulties, teachers tended to dissuade girls from aiming high in science. She believed that attitudes needed radical alteration in order to produce first-class scientists rather than competent laboratory assistants.

Twelve years later, in 1982, a survey in the journal New Scientist looked at the position of women in science and technology. Familiar points were made by the women surveyed: marriage and children had affected careers; teachers – and fathers – had an important influence in steering girls towards science, but teachers most often had provided well-meaning discouragement; woodwork, metalwork and engineering were rarely available as subjects for girls; only very bright pupils were encouraged to take

‘

Puzzle: A doctor and his son were in a traffic accident. The father was killed and the young man seriously injured. In hospital, the young man was prepared for surgery on the operating table. The surgeon cried in recognition, 'My God, this patient is my son.' Who was the surgeon?
Answer: Of course, the surgeon is his mother.

’

Boys and girls as a percentage of entrants for A level GCE, 1985 (England and Wales)

Source: Department of Education and Science and Welsh Joint Education Commitee

Physics

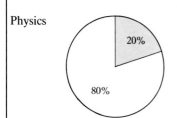

Computer Studies

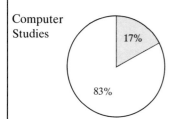

Chemistry

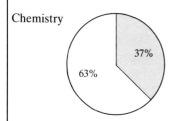

Maths

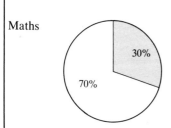

Biology

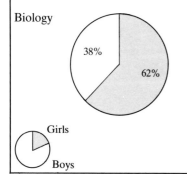

physics and chemistry; careers advisors often suggested nursing or teaching for girls, being astonished when asked for advice on nuclear physics or engineering.

At university, women science students were dismayed by the lack of women lecturers and other women students. They felt male teachers were not interested in them. At work many felt they were not taken seriously and were not regarded as competent to give technical advice.

Women responding to the 1982 survey were remembering situations as they existed ten or twenty years ago. The tables shown here compare a few more up-to-date statistics.

Contemporary figures are also worth noting. A study by Isobel Allen, published in 1988, on doctors and their careers (*Any Room at the Top?*) showed that, whereas by the 1990s women will make up fifty per cent of students entering medical schools, only thirteen per cent of hospital consultants are women (according to 1987 figures). Women doctors, it seems, have some way to go to reach equal status with their male colleagues.

Engineering, which until recently remained practically a male-only preserve, is still the most unlikely area of science to be entered by women. In 1984, a campaign called WISE (Women into Science and Engineering) was set up by the Equal Opportunities Commission and The Engineering Council to encourage more girls into a scientific or technical career. (Of the 300,000 engineers registered with the Council in 1985, about 530 were women.) At a time when both teaching and industry require more qualified scientists and

Comparison of men and women entering universities and polytechnics as undergraduates

Source: The Engineering Council

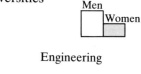

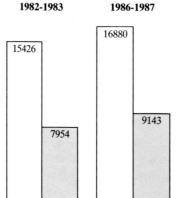

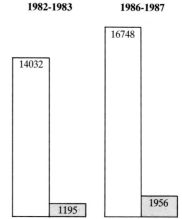

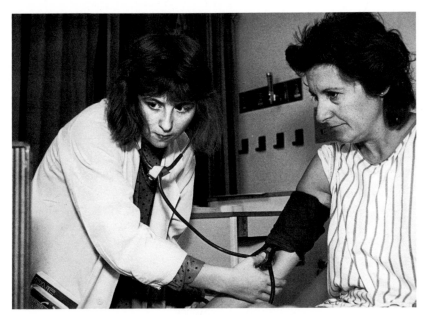

Left *A junior hospital doctor takes a patient's blood pressure. Nearly as many women as men now qualify as doctors in Britain, but as yet there are far fewer female than male consultants.*

engineers, particularly in areas of new technology, WISE has taken practical steps to improve the position.

Amendments to school courses and examinations have been introduced, including 'AS' levels (science study combined with arts); a career-break scheme has been launched, encouraging employers to keep in touch with female employees bringing up families; good practice in the classroom is emphasized (equal access for boys and girls to school computers, for example). Further education courses by which women from arts backgrounds can enter science and engineering have been established; links between schools and local engineering firms are encouraged.

Women scientists are gradually achieving a higher profile. They appear on television: notably Heather Couper (astronomer) and Miriam Stoppard (doctor); they help to present the science programme *Tomorrow's World*. And yet, the idea lingers that *real* scientists are male, with one or two brilliant female exceptions.

Among the general public the name of Jeffrey Archer, writer and politician, is well known. Less famous is his wife, Mary, the distinguished scientist – a former research fellow at the Royal Institution, fellow and lecturer in chemistry at Cambridge University, expert in solar energy. The female tradition in science is long, but mainly unknown; the work of many women scientists has been forgotten, ignored, taken over, or been assigned to others. Not until creative scientific work is associated as readily with women as it now is with men, will others feel confident enough to join the scientific world – and the possible contribution of these women to science will remain a lost one.

Elizabeth Berry (b. 1965)

In the past year, Liz Berry has worked for Michael Jackson in Rome and George Michael in Rotterdam. Thanks to her, the singers' concerts were spectacular visually as well as musically, for Liz is a lighting engineer – a 'troubleshooter' sent to venues throughout Europe by her company, which is one of the largest suppliers of automated lighting equipment in the world.

Liz (whose mother is a teacher and whose father is a mechanical engineer) did not much enjoy school, although she left with 'A' levels in English, biology and mathematics. She began studying for an English degree at Manchester University, but never completed the course. In her second year she discovered the Student Union concert PA (public address) system – and became in-house sound and lighting technician for rock concerts held in the student union building.

When she found how much she enjoyed the technical aspects of operating a sound and lighting system, she left university, despite

> '*I get some funny looks and comments when I turn up at a show clutching my little red toolbox to sort out a problem. There is definitely some resistance to the idea of a woman saving the show. The hardest part can be getting access to the backstage area – one security guard practically accused me of being a groupie.* Elizabeth Berry, 1988.'

her parents' anxiety. Armed with her maths 'A' level, she found an electronics course for students with a mixed arts/science background at the Polytechnic of the South Bank in London. Backed by WISE (Women into Science and Engineering) and the European Community, which paid Liz's grant, the one-year course was for women only.

Expecting 'man-hating feminists in dungarees', Liz found instead that her fellow students were an ordinary mixed bunch of ex-arts students, science graduates training for a practical skill, and students straight from school. She got her job through an advertisement.'It's not all glamour and the hours can be horrific, because the show must go on.' But Liz enjoys the work with live bands, the travel and the electronics. Soon she will leave the workshop where she is based to join the lighting systems road crew as it tours Europe.

Liz has been lucky to find a career which is fulfilling. She would like to see more women in science and engineering 'but there seems to be so little interest. On my HNC course they were unable to fill all the places. In my current job I have seen numerous positions advertised, including my replacement, but there has not been a single female applicant. What can be done about that?'

Liz Berry enjoys her job as a sound and lighting technician. She thinks it's a pity more women don't train for the job, which can be challenging and fun.

Projects

Women and science at school

1. In your school, how many girls took GCSE exams last year in each of the following subjects: physics, chemistry, mathematics, biology? How many boys took these subjects? How do the figures compare?

2. Ask your teacher to find out what the figures were five years ago for either GCE 'O' level or CSE exams at your school. Were they much different from those for last year?

3. How many science teachers are there in your school? How many of them are women? Can you work out what percentage they are of the total?

4. Do a careers survey among the members of your class. How many students want a career needing scientific qualifications? How many of these are boys? How many are girls?

5. What do the results of your surveys tell you about women and science at your school?

6. Some people think that girls do better at science when working in single-sex groups. Would you agree?

Women and science in the community

1. Ask each member of your family to describe their idea of a scientist. Ask them to name six famous scientists. Did anybody describe or name a woman? If so, whom?

2. Try to find out the names of doctors who are GPs in your neighbourhood. (Ask at your local library where you can look up the names.) How many of them are women, and how many are men?

3. In your family, who usually
a) mends a fuse?
b) wires a plug for an electrical appliance?
c) changes a light bulb?
d) programmes the washing machine?
Do the answers surprise you?

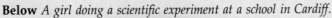

Below *A girl doing a scientific experiment at a school in Cardiff.*

Glossary

Atom Smallest part of an element.

Algebra Method of doing calculations by using letters as symbols for quantities.

Antibiotic Drug which can destroy germs causing infectious disease.

Anatomy Study of the structure of animals and plants.

Anthropology Study of humankind.

Apothecary Someone who prepares and sells drugs.

Apparatus In science, the instruments and tools used in a laboratory.

Archaeology Scientific study of human history through relics of the past.

Benzene Substance in coal-tar discovered by Michael Faraday in 1825. It is used to produce dyes.

Biophysics Form of biology which uses the techniques of physics in its studies.

Birth control Precautions taken against getting pregnant.

Botany Study of plants.

Calculus Branch of mathematics invented by Isaac Newton and Gottfried von Leibniz.

Cotton gin Machine for separating seeds from raw cotton.

Civil engineer Engineer who plans roads, railways, docks, harbours etc.

DNA Abbreviation for deoxyribonucleic acid, which carries the genetic 'code' that decides which characteristics an offspring inherits from its parents.

Element In chemistry, a substance that cannot be broken down into simpler substances. An element contains only one kind of atom.

Entomology Study of insects.

Evolution In biology, the process by which life has developed on earth.

Excavating Digging out. In archaeology a 'dig' uncovers human relics.

Folk medicine Traditional, 'unofficial' medicine.

Forceps Pincer-like surgical instrument.

Fossil Prehistoric remains of animal or plant, hardened into stone.

Genetics Study of heredity, or how characteristics are passed on from generation to generation.

Geology Study of rocks in the earth's crust.

Geometry Branch of mathematics dealing with lines, points, solids and surfaces.

Heredity Passing on of characteristics from parents to offspring.

Hermaphrodite Both male and female in one body.

Horticulture Gardening or market gardening, producing fruit and vegetables.

Industrial Revolution Period between about 1760–1840 in Britain, when industrial production increased as a result of technological innovations.

Inoculation Introducing a mild form of disease into the body to protect it against future infection.

Intellectual Person noted for the use of his or her mind.

Logarithms In mathematics, logarithm tables were used to help make calculations before the invention of electronic calculators.

Mechanics Study of forces acting on objects.

Midwifery Work carried out by midwives, to do with childbirth.

Mineralogy Study of minerals.

Molecule The basic particle of a substance.

Molluscs Group of soft-bodied animals without backbones, including slugs and snails.

Munitions Equipment and materials used in war, weapons.

Nebulae Clouds in space; sometimes galaxies of stars, sometimes dust and gas.

Nuclear fission and **fusion** Nuclear fission is a reaction in which a nucleus splits into two parts; nuclear fusion is a reaction in which atomic nuclei fuse to form a heavier nucleus.

Optics Study of light.

Palaeontology Study of **fossils.**

Pernicious anaemia Disease of the blood.

Quasar Source of radiation in space.

Royal Society An association founded in 1660 by Charles II to promote scientific research.

Specific gravity/relative density Ratio of the density of one substance to another, usually water.

Still Equipment for distilling liquids by turning them into vapour and back into liquid.

Technology Way science is put into practice.

Wireless telegraphy The sending of messages (usually Morse code) by radio waves.

Women's suffrage Right of women to vote in national elections.

Zoologist Student of animals.

Books to Read

Books for older readers

Alic, M. *Hypatia's Heritage* (The Women's Press, 1986)

Haber, L. *Women Pioneers of Science* (Harcourt Brace Jovanovich, 1979)

Levin, Beatrice S. *Women and Medicine* (Scarecrow Press, 1980)

Mozans, H.J. *Women in Science* (MIT Press, 1913, reprinted 1974)

Ogilvie, M.B. *Women in Science* (MIT Press, 1986)

Osen, L.M. *Women in Mathematics* (MIT Press, 1986)

Richter, D. *Women Scientists, The Road to Liberation* (Macmillan, 1982)

Sayre, Anne *Rosalind Franklin & DNA* (W.W. Norton & Company, 1978)

Books for younger readers

Alexander, Morag *A Woman's Place* (Wayland, 1983)

Birch, Beverly *Marie Curie: Radium Scientist* (Macdonald, 1988)

Bryan, Jenny *Health and Science* (Macdonald, 1988)

Dineen, J. *Twenty Inventors* (Wayland, 1988)

Goulds, Sharon *The Role of Women* (Macdonald, 1985)

Harris, Sarah *Women at Work* (Batsford, 1981)

McConnell, Eileen *Women* (Batsford, 1982)

Turner, D. *Florence Nightingale* (Wayland, 1986)

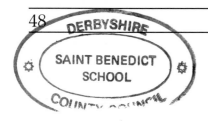

Index

Numbers in **bold** refer to illustrations.